THE LIBRARY OF
AMERICAN
LIVES AND TIMES™

ROBERT FULTON

and the Development of the Steamboat

Morris A. Pierce

The Rosen Publishing Group's
PowerPlus Books™
New York

For John J. Waters Jr.,
mentor and friend

Published in 2003 by The Rosen Publishing Group, Inc.
29 East 21st Street, New York, NY 10010

First Edition

*Editor's Note: All quotations have been reproduced as they appeared in
the letters and diaries from which they were borrowed. No correction was
made to the inconsistent spelling that was common in that time period.*

Library of Congress Cataloging-in-Publication Data

Pierce, Morris A.
Robert Fulton and the development of the steamboat / by Morris A.
Pierce.— 1st ed.
    p. cm. — (The library of American lives and times)
Includes bibliographical references (p.   ) and index.
ISBN 0-8239-5737-3 (library binding)
1. Fulton, Robert, 1765–1815—Juvenile literature. 2. Marine engi-
neers—United States—Biography—Juvenile literature. 3. Inventors—
United States—Biography—Juvenile literature. 4. Steamboats—United
States—History—19th century—Juvenile literature. [1. Fulton, Robert,
1765–1815. 2. Inventors. 3. Steamboats—History.] I. Title. II. Series.
VM140.F9 P53 2003
623.8'24'092—dc21

                    2001005541

Manufactured in the United States of America

CONTENTS

1. Childhood 1765–1780 5

2. Apprentice 1780–1787 .17

3. Artist 1787–1793 23

4. Canal Engineer 1793–1797 27

5. Submarines 1797–1802 .35

6. Steamboats 1802–1804 .49

7. Torpedoes 1804–1806 63

8. Pioneer 1806–1807 72

9. Entrepreneur 1807–1815 81

Timeline 100
Glossary 103
Additional Resources 107
Bibliography 108
Index 109

1. Childhood
1765–1780

Robert Fulton was born in the colony of Pennsylvania, part of British North America, on November 14, 1765. He died not quite a half century later in New York, then part of the United States of America. During his lifetime, he witnessed the American and the French Revolutions and helped to start the industrial and the transportation revolutions that transformed America's small agricultural economy into the richest nation on Earth.

Fulton's father, also named Robert, was a Scottish Presbyterian who had emigrated from Ireland to Pennsylvania in the early 1700s. His ancestors had moved from Scotland to Ireland in the seventeenth century, after the English had conquered Ireland. Times were difficult for the Scottish immigrants, though. The British parliament placed severe economic and legal restrictions on them. Like the Catholic Irish, the Presbyterian Scots were not allowed to hold office and

---

Opposite: Robert Fulton, who was born in 1765, would later study art with Benjamin West, as did many well-known artists from that time. Charles Willson Peale, a notable student of West, painted this portrait of Fulton in 1807, when Fulton was in his early forties.

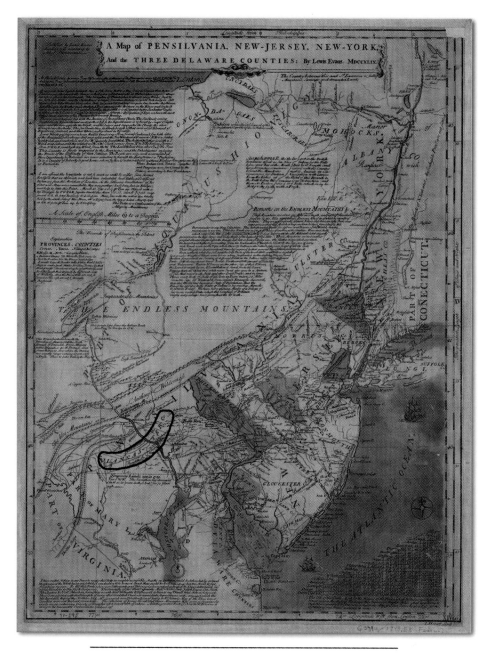

This map, created by L. Hebert and published by Lewis Evans
in 1749, shows Pennsylvania, New Jersey, New York, and
part of Delaware. Lancaster County, Pennsylvania, where
Fulton grew up, is circled in blue on the map.

had to pay taxes to support the Church of England. Many Scots, unable to prosper in Ireland, moved to America between 1714 and 1775. The journey across the Atlantic Ocean could be very grim. Food and drink were rationed, and the health and comfort of the passengers was of little concern. When the ship arrived in America, those who had enough money paid their fare and left. Healthy passengers who could not pay their fare were sold into indentured service to pay for their journey. Sick passengers were simply sold at auction. If one person in a family died, the rest of the family was responsible for that person's fare. Despite these conditions, the Scots felt they had arrived in the promised land. They settled in many areas, particularly in Pennsylvania and Maryland.

By 1735, Fulton Sr. was a tailor in Lancaster, Pennsylvania, the first inland town in America. He was active in civic affairs and was secretary of the local volunteer fire department. In 1759, he became a founding member of the Juliana Library Company (now the Lancaster County Library), the fourth-oldest public library in America. That same year, Fulton Sr. married Mary Smith, the daughter of a local farmer. Robert and Mary Fulton moved into a house on what is now Penn Square in Lancaster. They lived there for five years and had three daughters, Elizabeth, Isabella, and Mary, called by their nicknames, Betsy, Belle, and Polly.

Early in 1765, the Fultons sold their house in Lancaster and moved to a farm of more than 300 acres

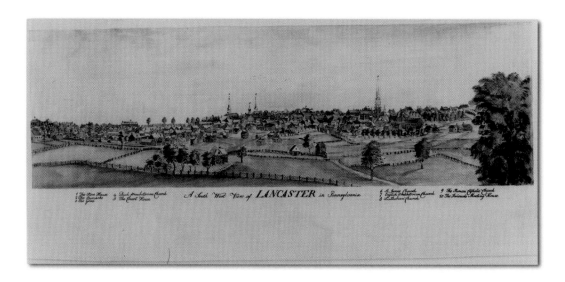

This hand-colored lithograph, published in 1929, shows a southwest view of Lancaster, Pennsylvania, around 1798. Many of the buildings labeled on this map are churches or meetinghouses, which reflects the religious and cultural diversity of Lancaster at this time.

(121 ha) on Conowingo Creek in Little Britain Township. The farm was 30 miles (48 km) south of Lancaster and 5 miles (8 km) north of Pennsylvania's border with Maryland. In November 1765, their son Robert was born. A year later, Abraham was born. The house was destroyed by a fire in 1822, but it was rebuilt and today is the Robert Fulton Birthplace museum.

Fulton Sr. had borrowed money to purchase the farm, but he was an unsuccessful farmer. In 1772, the farm was sold. Fulton Sr. moved his family back to Lancaster and resumed working as a tailor. He died suddenly two years later, leaving his widow to care for their five children. However sad these circumstances were, moving back to Lancaster was a crucial event in young Robert's life. Lancaster had a population of more than four thousand, and its rich mixture of culture and languages provided a much broader education than was available on a farm. The city was on the main road between Philadelphia and the Pennsylvania frontier. Cheap land and boundless opportunities attracted a constant stream of settlers, many traveling in Conestoga wagons built in Lancaster. The Fultons' neighbors included Swiss Mennonites, German Lutherans, Jewish fur traders,

Many families traveled west in covered wagons, such as the one depicted in this 1802 illustration drawn by George Beck and engraved by T. Cartwright. They hoped to take advantage of the cheap land and new opportunities that had opened up on the frontier.

The Society of Friends, as the Quakers were formally called, had been instrumental in founding Pennsylvania and ensuring that religious tolerance was the rule there. Other colonies were not as tolerant. In 1660, Mary Dyer and three of her Quaker brethren were hanged on Boston Common for refusing to leave the Puritan colony of Massachusetts. In Lancaster, at least fourteen religious denominations worshiped in quiet, if separate, harmony.

Huguenots, slaves, free blacks, and their own Scotch-Irish community. A wide range of merchants and artisans settled in Lancaster itself, prospering from the local trade.

The Fulton family was poor after the death of Fulton Sr., but with help from relatives, they were not destitute. Later in life, Robert wrote letters to his family that expressed warm memories of his childhood. Robert Fulton's mother took charge of her children's primary education, often reading books to them by the fire. Robert entered school at the age of eight knowing how to read, write, and do basic arithmetic. Caleb Johnson, his schoolmaster, was both a Tory and a Quaker. Unlike many colonists who disliked British rule, Tories were loyal to King George III and thought colonists had little cause for complaint.

Robert spent much time in the Juliana Library, which his father had helped to found. William Henry, a scientist and mechanic, was in charge of the library. He had opened a gun factory in Lancaster in 1750, and had supplied weapons for General Edward Braddock during the French and Indian War. A talented surveyor, Henry had also laid out a canal between Pennsylvania's Lehigh and Susquehanna Rivers and had built a working model of a steamboat. Young Robert apparently absorbed all that he saw, asserting when he was only ten that "his head was so full of original ideas that there was no room for the storage of the contents of dusty books."

Two years before Robert was born, the British had won the French and Indian War, expelling the French from North America. At one time New France had stretched from Montreal on the Saint Lawrence River in Canada through the Great Lakes and down the Mississippi River to New Orleans. After the French left, Canada and the territories around the Great Lakes became part of British North America, joining the thirteen colonies on the East Coast. Spain took control of the Louisiana Territory, including the Mississippi River and New Orleans. Many colonists saw the departure of the French as a chance to expand into the American frontier. The British government, however, had signed a treaty with the Native American tribes in 1763, limiting

This 1755 French map of North America shows the boundary between French and American territories. The French territories are in green. The American territories would later become states in the new United States of America. Louisiana (spelled Louisiane on the map) would be sold to the United States in 1803.

*After winning the French and Indian War,
the British government established a
boundary between the British colonies along
the coast and the Indian territories on the
western side of the Appalachian Mountains.
By royal proclamation, in 1763, a line was
drawn down the Appalachians marking the
limit of settlement from the British colonies,
beyond which Indian trade was to be conducted
strictly through British-appointed commissioners.
The proclamation, which sprang in part from
a respect for Indian rights, caused concern
among British colonists for two reasons.
It meant that limits were being set to the
prospects of settlement and speculation in
western lands, and it took control of these lands
out of colonial hands. The most ambitious men
in the colonies saw the proclamation as a
loss of power to control their own fortunes.*

expansion of the colonies to a Proclamation Line along the crest of the Allegheny Mountains. British soldiers kept the colonists within the treaty boundaries. Although colonists such as schoolmaster Caleb Johnson were untroubled and perhaps even comforted by the presence of British troops, many other colonists saw the troops as a threat to liberty.

Resentment against the British king increased after several bad decisions were made by ministers in London, thousands of miles (km) away. British parliament passed several unpopular acts and taxed the colonists to pay for troops stationed in America. The colonists were outraged. Many refused to pay the taxes because they had no representation in Parliament. Riots and protests became increasingly common throughout the colonies. Finally the Boston Massacre, in 1770, and the Boston Tea Party, in 1773, pushed the colonists to the brink of war. In April 1775, British troops marched on Lexington and Concord, and the American Revolution began.

The outbreak of revolution was an enormous adventure for a ten-year-old boy of insatiable curiosity such as Robert Fulton. Although Lancaster saw no actual fighting during the war, it was still full of action. The town was flooded with refugees from Philadelphia after the British captured that city in September 1777. These refugees included the writer and inventor Thomas Paine and the astronomer David Rittenhouse. Lancaster was the nation's capital for a day on September 27, 1777, when

W. D. Cooper's *Boston Tea Party* engraving was printed in
The History of North America, published in 1789. In this work the
colonists, poorly disguised as Native Americans, can be seen dump-
ing the 342 crates of tea into the harbor on December 16, 1773.

the Continental Congress held a session there. The town
was also a major supply center for the Continental army
and held thousands of British and Hessian prisoners of
war. Some outspoken Tories, including Caleb Johnson,
ended up in jail as well.

Even during this unsettled time, Robert's inventive
talents were clear. From an early age he made his own
lead pencils, an air gun, and a boat with mechanical
paddles. He experimented with mercury, then known as
quicksilver, and his friends called him Quicksilver Bob.
In 1778, when the Lancaster town council forbade the

Here Fulton has sketched a boat with paddles, an idea he had conceived when he was a young boy. This is his first sketch of such a boat, done in 1793. This particular print is from a duplicate in the possession of Charles, third Earl Stanhope.

practice of lighting scarce candles to celebrate Independence Day, Robert told a friend he was going to build a skyrocket "to illuminate the heavens instead of the streets." When his friend said this was impossible, Robert replied, "No, sir; there is nothing impossible."

After a long struggle, the American Revolution ended successfully for the colonists. Just as America was entering a new era as an independent nation, Robert Fulton was on his way to a wider world.

2. Apprentice 1780–1787

Around the age of fifteen, Fulton was apprenticed to a silversmith in Philadelphia. Many young men and women learned trades through apprenticeship, in which a master craftsperson agreed to instruct a young worker and to provide him or her food, clothing, and shelter. In return the worker agreed to bind himself or herself to the master for a set period of time. After that period of time was finished, the successful apprentice became a journeyman working for wages, or even a master in charge of a business. Apprentices were sometimes treated harshly, and many colonists told horror stories about their bad experiences. Although silversmithing was a highly regarded occupation, Fulton liked neither the work nor his subordinate position as an apprentice. Nonetheless his talented hands learned valuable new skills as he was introduced into an entirely new world of art, intellect, commerce, and society.

When Fulton's apprenticeship was completed, he set up his own business as a painter of miniature portraits. These were often done on ivory and were very popular for lockets and rings. Fulton probably received instruction in painting from Charles Willson Peale, one of the most prominent artists in America in the 1700s and the 1800s, and the founder of the Pennsylvania Academy of the Fine Arts. Fulton also learned how to make elaborate jewelry from human hair, which requires great dexterity and patience.

Fulton is known to have painted eight miniatures, two large oil portraits, and two landscapes during this period. One of the people who sat for Fulton's miniature portraits was Benjamin Franklin. Franklin had served as American minister to France during the

Robert Fulton painted these miniatures of Edward R. Martin and Margaretta James Martin between 1800 and 1810. Wealthy individuals often commissioned miniature portraits that would be used much like family photographs today. The portraits' small scale made them difficult to create.

American Revolution. He returned to Philadelphia in September 1785. A true American hero, Franklin tirelessly promoted science and engineering, which he believed would be necessary for the success of the new nation. Philadelphia, then the largest city in America, was already the country's center for scientific study. Organizations such as the American Philosophical Society encouraged scientific inquiry in a wide range of fields. Christopher Colles, who had built a steam engine to supply water to New York City before the American Revolution, taught classes for mechanics. Thomas Paine, famous for his revolutionary writings, exhibited a model of a cast-iron, single-span bridge at Franklin's house. Franklin presented his own ideas for boats propelled by steam and corresponded with John Fitch, who demonstrated a steamboat in Philadelphia in August 1787.

Although painting remained Fulton's first interest, he could not have failed to be caught up in the general scientific excitement in Philadelphia. Early in 1786, however, Fulton became ill with tuberculosis, then a common disease in crowded cities. He escaped the unhealthy atmosphere of Philadelphia for the clear mountain air of Warm Springs in Bath, Virginia (now Berkeley Springs), a rustic yet fashionable resort overlooking the upper Potomac River. One of the frequent visitors to Warm Springs was George Washington, former commander in chief of the Continental army. Washington believed that improving transportation to

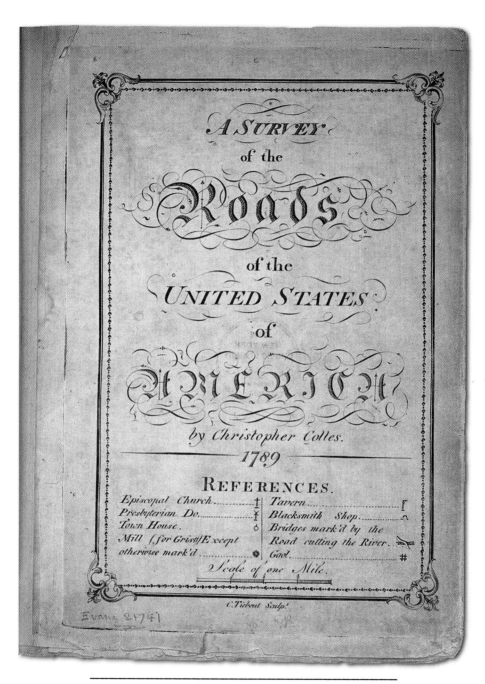

Christopher Colles was a well-known scientist in the late 1700s. In 1789, he wrote *A Survey of the Roads of the United States of America*, pictured here. This was the first American road guide. It was modeled after the English road guides of the 1700s and based on maps prepared under Washington's orders during the American Revolution.

the territory west of the Allegheny Mountains was essential to the prosperity of the new nation. He thought the Potomac River was the best route between the eastern seaboard and the Ohio River valley. Along with several other men, Washington formed the Patowmack Company to make the Potomac River navigable by small boats. The greatest obstacle was the Great Falls of the Potomac, where the water drops 76 feet (23 m) in only 1,250 yards (1.1 km). Washington hired engineer James Rumsey to design and build a canal around the Great Falls. Rumsey lived in Bath when Fulton visited there, and Fulton undoubtedly learned about the five locks Rumsey designed on the Potomac Canal. Construction had been underway for a year when Fulton visited Bath in 1786, and it would not be complete until 1801.

His health restored, Fulton returned to Philadelphia, where he reopened his shop and advertised himself as a

Benjamin West, shown here in a 1781 portrait by Gilbert Stuart, was an influential artist in both America and Europe. He went to England in 1763 and stayed there for the rest of his life.

painter of miniatures and hair worker. He had also decided to study painting in London. He obtained a letter, probably from Benjamin Franklin, introducing Fulton to Benjamin West, a leading artist in London who had lived near Lancaster. Franklin himself had studied printing in London and had encouraged young Americans to study abroad. Before he left, Fulton visited his mother in Lancaster and bought her a small farm. He also bought three building lots for his siblings. One of the greatest mysteries about Fulton's life is how he accumulated the money to purchase this land and an even larger sum to travel and to live in England. Clearly he had a benefactor, whose identity remains unknown to us. In any event, during the summer of 1787, the tall, handsome, twenty-one-year-old Fulton sailed to London and to a future he could scarcely have imagined. He would not return to America for twenty years, and he never saw his mother again.

3. Artist 1787–1793

Robert Fulton's journey across the Atlantic Ocean in a sailing ship undoubtedly took several weeks. The trip may have been uneventful, since he never wrote about the journey or passed any details of it along to friends. London, with a population of 700,000, was the largest English-speaking city in the world. Though Philadelphia, with 40,000 citizens, was by no means small, London would have been an entirely new world for the young American. He presented himself to the painter Benjamin West at West's studio on Newman Street and passed along news of Benjamin Franklin, William Henry, and Charles Willson Peale. Fulton rented a room from painter Robert Davy on Charlotte Street. Life as an artist in London was hard, but Fulton made many friends.

Fulton's life was filled with uncertainty as he realized the enormous difficulties of becoming a successful artist in a city full of artists. Despite his many friends, he spent many solitary hours and was perhaps even homesick occasionally. Correspondence with his family and friends back in America was expensive, and often

London, pictured here in an engraving from the 1780s, had a population of 700,000 by the time of Fulton's arrival. This was more than seventeen times Philadelphia's population at the time.

months passed before a reply was received. Postage was based on weight and was paid by a letter's recipient, so Fulton asked his mother "to write close and small" on thin stationery. In 1789, Fulton was admitted to the highly respected Royal Academy of Arts, the best art school in London. Before entering the school, he toured France for three months to view the art of the French. After returning to London, he diligently pursued his studies, and in 1791, he displayed two paintings at a Royal Academy exhibition and four others at The

London Society of Artists. These paintings led to an invitation to paint the portrait of Viscount William Courtenay. Fulton traveled to Courtenay's estate, Powderham Castle, near Exeter in southwest England. Courtenay was very pleased with the portrait. Fulton was recommended by the Viscount to his friends. Fulton stayed at Powderham for eighteen months.

In 1793, he returned to London and exhibited four paintings at the Royal Academy. His patron and friend West had recently been elected president of the academy, a post he held for nearly three decades. After the exhibition, Fulton returned to the west of England, staying at the town of Torquay on the English Channel.

The Royal Academy of Arts is an old and prestigious organization that has existed in England since 1768. In 1868, the Royal Academy of Arts moved to Burlington House, where it remains today. Note the grand entrance shown above.

He continued to paint, including a scene of British naval ships in nearby Tor Bay preparing for war with France. The 1793 exhibition, however, had earned him neither honors nor new customers. At some point, he realized that his destiny did not rest with painting. Using his mechanical skills, he built an improved machine for cutting and polishing marble that received a silver medal from the prestigious Royal Society for the Encouragement of Arts, Manufactures and Commerce in 1794. Fulton continued to paint for the rest of his life, but it was no longer his primary career. Rather than struggle to become a painter in a world filled with expert, famous, and competing artists, Fulton decided that his mechanical talents offered many more opportunities in a world where engineers were few.

4. Canal Engineer
1793–1797

During his stay at Powderham Castle, Fulton met several of Courtenay's friends and neighbors, including Francis Egerton, duke of Bridgewater, and Charles, third Earl Stanhope. One of the concerns of these men was the poor state of transportation in England. English roads, although better than the roads of other countries, were incredibly bad. Transport of passengers and freight was expensive and slow. Many seaports served coastal areas, but internal navigation was limited to only a few rivers, including the Thames, the Trent, the Severn, the Avon, and the Great Ouse. In 1750, England had only 1,000 miles (1,609 km) of navigable waterways. In 1759, the wealthy duke visited the Canal du Midi in France. This canal, or artificial river, was built in the 1660s to allow boats to travel from the Atlantic Ocean to the Mediterranean Sea. The duke

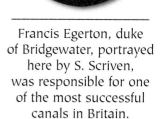

Francis Egerton, duke of Bridgewater, portrayed here by S. Scriven, was responsible for one of the most successful canals in Britain.

This map from around 1815, *Wallis's New Travelling Map of England and Wales* . . . , shows clearly the main roads as well as the rivers that were used for transportation in England at this time. The map also marks the distances between markets by river or by road. It reflects the greater reliance on rivers for transportation after 1765.

decided that a similar canal would allow coal from his mines near Manchester to be delivered to the port of Liverpool at very low cost. His Bridgewater Canal opened in 1765, to great success. The age of canals in England was underway.

Numerous other canals were built, and many more were proposed in the next decades. One of great interest to Courtenay and to Stanhope was the Bude Canal. Designed to link the seaport of Bude on the Bristol Channel with the Tamar River, this canal would allow boats to travel from the Bristol Channel to the English Channel without traveling on the open sea. The canal would pass through land owned by both men, allowing them to transport goods more economically. It was to be 75 miles (121 km) long and rise to a summit 484 feet (148 m) above sea level. The Bude Canal Committee proposed using traditional locks in the lower section, but the lack of water at higher levels led them to propose attaching wheels to the canal boats. The boats would then be placed on rails and be pulled by horses to the next canal section.

The Bude Canal Committee issued its report in October 1793. Fulton immediately sent its chairman, Stanhope, a plan he felt was more efficient. Fulton suggested using inclined planes rather than locks and horse-drawn railways. Although his idea was considered, it was not adopted. Despite the rejection of his idea, Fulton applied for a patent to protect it, which was awarded in June 1794. A patent gave exclusive rights to use an

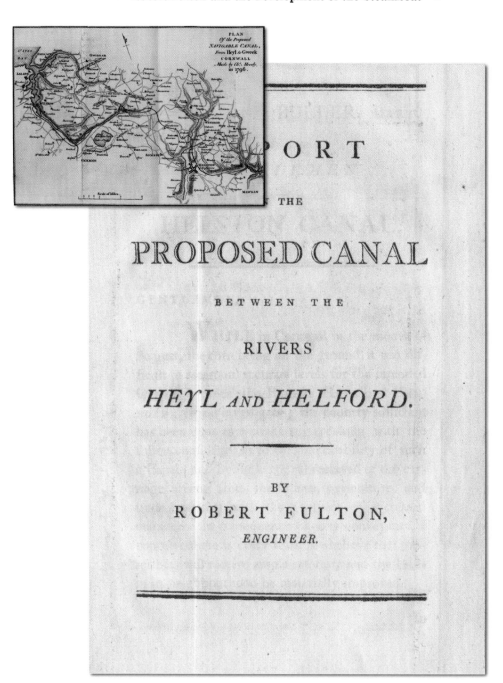

ORT

THE

PROPOSED CANAL

BETWEEN THE

RIVERS

HEYL AND *HELFORD.*

BY

ROBERT FULTON,

ENGINEER.

Fulton wrote *Report on the Proposed Canal Between the Rivers Heyl and Helford* in 1793. The book is pictured here with an inset of one of the maps he drew to illustrate his own plan. He thought it would make more sense to use inclined planes rather than a system of locks.

invention for fourteen years. Patents were very expensive to obtain and only about sixty were issued each year by the government. Later that year, Fulton visited several canals around Manchester, including the duke of Bridgewater's canal, the most profitable in Britain. While in Manchester, Fulton obtained a contract with the Peak Forest Company, which was planning a canal to connect lime quarries and kilns to the canal network around Manchester. Fulton might also have seen a demonstration of a steam-powered boat on the Bridgewater Canal during the fall of 1794. He wrote a letter to Boulton and Watt, a company that made steam engines, requesting information on a small steam engine to power a boat, but they did not respond. He and Stanhope also corresponded about their mutual interest in steamboats.

Fulton then devised a machine to reduce the tremendous amount of hand labor involved in digging canals. Pulled by four horses, the machine would scoop up soil and would toss it to the side. Although it was a workable idea, Fulton was unable to find a market for it. He then turned his attention to aqueduct structures, which allowed canals to cross rivers and valleys. Fulton proposed a much longer span than had been used previously. The Peak Forest Company was impressed by his design, and their chief engineer wrote a report praising it, but in the end, they did not use it on their canal. Fulton's design, however, was utilized several years later on the beautiful Pontcysyllte Aqueduct, which carried

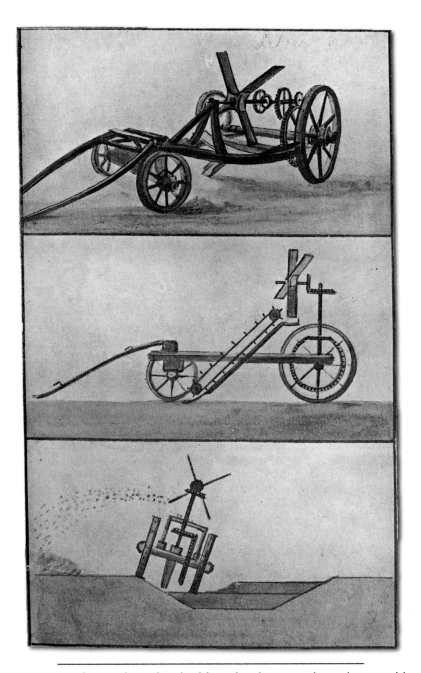

In 1796, Robert Fulton sketched his idea for a machine that would make digging canals easier. It would be pulled by horses as it scooped up dirt and tossed it aside. His original drawing was reprinted in H. W. Dickinson's *Robert Fulton, Engineer and Artist; His Life and Works*.

the Ellesmere Canal over the River Dee in Wales. Completed in 1805, it is the world's tallest canal aqueduct at 125 feet (38 m) high and 1,007 feet (307 m) long.

Impressed with his skill and ideas, the Peak Forest Company paid Fulton well and also offered to pay for printing a book about Fulton's plan for a network of small canals. He accepted enthusiastically and began writing a book to build his reputation as a canal engineer. He first advertised his basic principles in a newspaper and invited other engineers to respond, so that he could produce the most accurate work. He then took six months to produce 150 pages of text and several detailed drawings illustrating the principles of his plan. His book, *A Treatise on the Improvement of Canal Navigation*, was published in March 1796, and it was widely read. Although primarily aimed at readers in England, it also described a proposed 350-mile (563-km) canal to connect Philadelphia to Pittsburgh in Pennsylvania.

Robert Fulton's excellent book enhanced his engineering reputation, but it did not make him any money. England was in the middle of a financial crisis caused by the war with France, and Fulton received only one small contract to survey a canal. Failing to make his fortune in England, Fulton turned his eyes back to America. He sent a copy of the book to George Washington, who was just completing his second term as president. Washington sent a gracious reply, but he did not devote any time to canal development.

Fulton continued to work on his plan for a Pennsylvanian canal and actively sought investors. In April 1797, he sold one-fourth of the project to John Barker Church, brother-in-law of Alexander Hamilton. Under the arrangement with Church, the plan was expanded beyond the Pennsylvania project. Fulton was to go to Paris, secure a French patent for his idea of small canals, and actively promote their construction in France. Church would return to America and would obtain additional investors there. Intending to stay in France for only six months before returning to America, Fulton crossed the English Channel in June 1797, to begin yet another adventure in his remarkable life.

5. Submarines
1797–1802

Robert Fulton had first visited Paris in 1790, just months after the start of the French Revolution. On his second visit seven years later, France was ruled by the Directory, whose strongest personality was General Napoléon Bonaparte. France had been at war with Britain for four years and, under Napoléon's leadership, would soon send French armies across Europe.

Benjamin West had given Fulton a letter of introduction to fellow American Joel Barlow, who was living in Paris. Barlow was a well-known writer and had been made a French citizen for his strong support of the French Revolution. In 1795, Barlow was appointed American minister to Algiers, in Africa. There he negotiated several treaties with the Barbary States, which had been terrorizing American shipping. Barlow also secured the release of captured American sailors. Fulton got along well with

Next page: In 1783, America had just won the revolution against Britain with the help of France. Soon France would have a revolution of its own. Fulton arrived in Paris, which is shown here in a 1783 map, months after this revolution had begun. Fulton used the changes in the French government to promote his inventions.

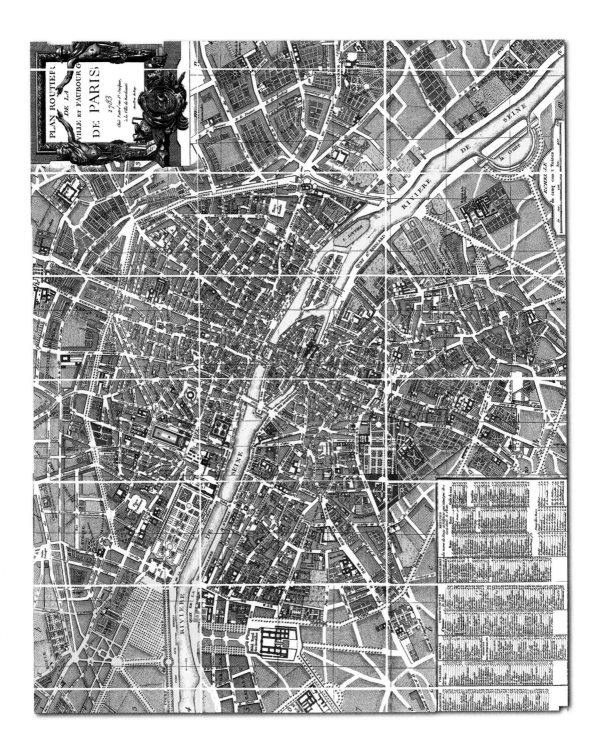

Barlow and his wife, Ruth, and lived with them for several years. Fulton worked hard to promote his canal project. He received a French patent, emphasizing the sound financial principles and the republican values that his canals would bring to France. His canal plans, however, were soon overshadowed by the situation between France and Britain. In December 1797, he delivered to the French government a plan for his latest endeavor, submarines that could "annihilate the British Navy."

Considering that Fulton had lived in England for more than ten years and had made many friends there, his plan to destroy the British navy could be seen, at the very least, as ungracious and perhaps even as treacherous. However, Fulton's larger purpose was to introduce a weapon so destructive that it would make war too terrible to be fought. Unfortunately it didn't turn out that way. In the end submarines were widely used in the twentieth century to sink passenger ships as well as cargo and naval vessels, killing thousands of people. Fulton also apparently failed to consider that French relations with America were severely strained by an American treaty with England. French and American naval forces clashed repeatedly before a settlement was negotiated in October 1800. Fulton's submarine could easily have been used against American shipping. In addition to all of this, surprise attacks were illegal under international law, and any submarine crewmen captured would be subject to execution as common criminals.

Robert Fulton painted this portrait of his friend Joel Barlow
in 1805. Barlow, born in Connecticut, lived from 1754 to 1812
and was quite a well-known writer. He was believed also to
write collectively with David Humphreys, John Trumbull, Timothy
Dwight, and others who called themselves the Hartford Wits.

Whatever other motives Fulton had, the primary purpose of his submarine plan was to bring him both fame and fortune. His plan required no investment by the French government, as he would be paid only after the submarine sank enemy warships, but he felt assured of its success. The French navy minister was intrigued by the concept, which already had a long history. Dutch inventor Cornelis Drebbel had demonstrated a successful submarine in the 1620s to an astonished crowd along the River Thames. In 1776, American David Bushnell had built an underwater vessel named the *Turtle* that attacked three British warships. Bushnell's craft was

David Bushnell's *Turtle*, created in 1776, is shown in this painting by E. Tufnell. Governor Trumbull of Connecticut and General George Washington supported Bushnell's submarine project. Washington said on September 26, 1776, "Bushnell is a man of great mechanical powers, fertile in invention and a master of execution." Unfortunately his attack on the HMS *Eagle* and the other British ships was not successful.

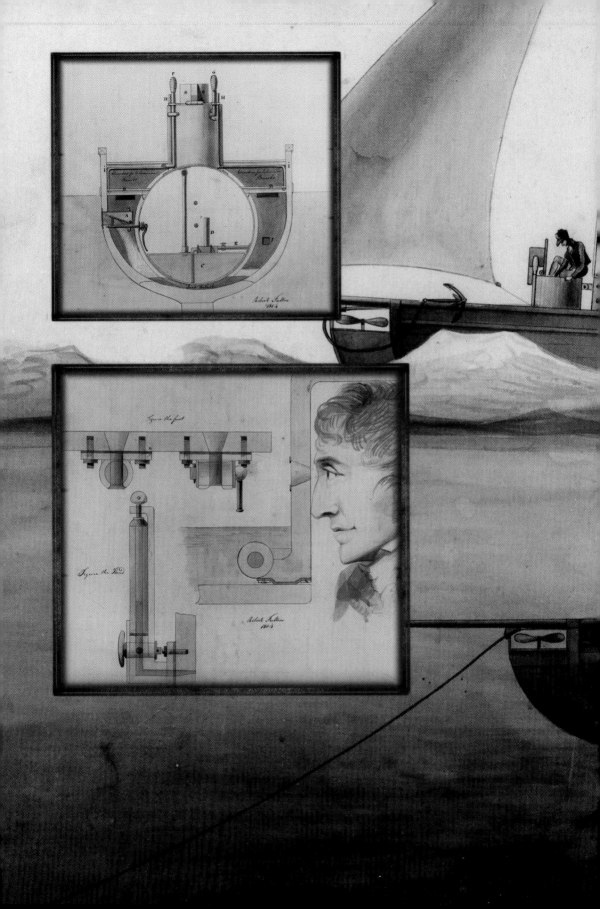

designed to attach an explosive to a warship's wooden hull, but the craft was virtually impossible to maneuver while submerged and the attacks were unsuccessful.

In Fulton's design for the *Nautilus,* the submarine required a crew of three, was 21 feet (6 m) long, and was slightly more than 6 feet (2 m) wide in the middle. On the surface it was powered by a sail, and under water it was driven by a hand-cranked screw propeller. The crew worked by candlelight, which consumed the scarce oxygen inside the vessel. The *Nautilus's* method of attack was identical to the one in Bushnell's design, but the ability to submerge for three hours, compared to the *Turtle's* thirty minutes, made the *Nautilus* a much more viable machine. Despite a thorough review of the plans by French officials and strong support from the navy minister, the government rejected the scheme.

His plans once again frustrated, Fulton thought about returning to America but stayed in Paris. He improved the *Nautilus's* design, built a large model, and pestered various officials with letters and documents. His efforts were successful enough that a commission was appointed to examine the model and the plans. They first met on August 7, 1798, unaware that Admiral Horatio Nelson had sunk Napoléon's fleet in the harbor of Alexandria,

Previous Spread: The collage shows various sketches by Robert Fulton of the *Nautilus.* The top left image, made in 1806, is a cross section showing the interior chambers for the crew, ballast, and bombs. The bottom left image shows the periscope. The image in the background is an external view of the submarine and the periscope, one an underwater view and one a view as it sails on the surface.

Egypt, only days earlier. The commission, which included the well-known French manufacturer Auguste Charles Périer, was pleased with Fulton's craft. They recommended he build a full-scale prototype with slight changes, but despite Fulton's impatience, the French government was not yet ready to proceed with this "terrible means of destruction."

Despite Fulton's living frugally in Paris, his submarine project had left him seriously in debt. He cast about for other ways to make money. He invented and patented a rope-making machine. He also built a panorama to entertain Parisians, copying and improving on one he had seen in London. The panorama was a large, circular room with an uninterrupted painting of a landscape along the outside wall and a raised viewing platform. The painting was on a large canvas that was slowly turned so it moved past the viewers. The first production was a bird's-eye view of Paris, which he received permission to paint from the roof of the Tuileries Palace. He hired four painters and gave them precise instructions on perspective and scale. It was an immediate commercial success and a second one was built, connected by a small arcade. The Passages des Panoramas, as the arcade was called, still exists today, although the panoramas themselves were demolished in 1831. Fulton sold the panoramas and received a small sum for each ticket sold.

Fulton continued to work on his canal scheme, and his *Treatise* was published in a French translation in the

The Passages des Panoramas, as the arcade was called, still exists today, although the panoramas themselves were demolished in 1831. The arcade was built to connect Fulton's panoramas.

spring of 1799. No canal work was planned due to the war, so Fulton redoubled his efforts to promote the *Nautilus*. Despite gaining more support, nothing came of the project, and Fulton threatened to take his invention elsewhere. This crude tactic worked. In early October 1799, the French naval minister personally came to Fulton's lodgings to examine the model. The minister recommended that the project would be cheaper than rebuilding the fleet, which had not been very successful against the English. Napoléon returned from the military

In this famous 1801 painting by Jacques-Louis David, Napoléon is pictured in 1800 when he led his forces over the snowy Great Saint Bernard Pass into Italy to attack the Austrian army in Genoa.

campaign in Egypt on October 16, 1799. Napoléon proceeded to overthrow the government and became first consul. He became, for all practical purposes, a dictator. Although Fulton had not received a contract from the French government, he hired Périer to build the *Nautilus*, which was demonstrated to a large crowd along the Seine River on June 13, 1800. Fulton and his assistant, Nathaniel Sargent, submerged the *Nautilus* for nearly twenty minutes and it surfaced some distance away. Then they repeated the demonstration and returned to the starting point before demonstrating the use of sails to move the craft on the surface. Both the naval minister and the crowd were ecstatic, and further tests were ordered at Rouen, farther down the Seine River. The currents there were very difficult, and Fulton suggested the tests be conducted at Le Havre, a seaport from which action against the British fleet could be conducted.

Fulton made further improvements to his craft and experimented with a new method of attacking enemy ships using a floating mine, an idea first demonstrated by Bushnell in Philadelphia. After further attempts to gain the government's approval, Fulton was surprised when orders arrived in Le Havre granting his requests. Shortly thereafter Fulton made the *Nautilus* ready for war, and two attempts were made to attack English warships. During one Fulton kept his submarine submerged for six hours. In both cases, the ships escaped from the submarine unharmed. Facing harsh weather in the Channel, Fulton secured the *Nautilus* for the winter and returned to Paris. He wrote a detailed account of what had happened and recommended construction of an even larger submarine, 30 feet (9 m) long. He was also granted an interview with Napoléon, during which Fulton probably demonstrated his model in a tank of water. The first consul was not enthusiastic, however, and even the support of the naval minister was fading, perhaps because the attacks had failed. Nevertheless Napoléon agreed to give Fulton additional funds to continue work on the *Nautilus*, but not to build the larger submarine.

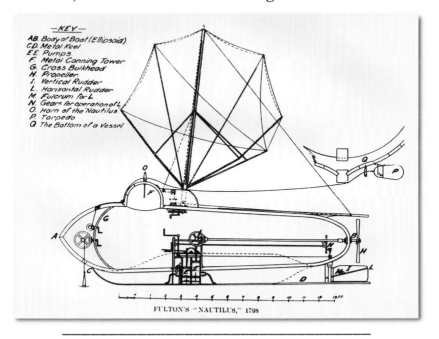

—KEY—
AB. Body of Boat (Ellipsoid)
CD. Metal Keel
EE. Pumps
F. Metal Conning Tower
G. Cross Bulkhead
H. Propeller
I. Vertical Rudder
L. Horizontal Rudder
M. Fulcrum for L
N. Gears for operation of L
O. Horn of the 'Nautilus'
P. Torpedo
Q. The Bottom of a Vessel

FULTON'S "NAUTILUS," 1798

Fulton made drawings of the new additions to the *Nautilus* in 1798, including a tank of compressed oxygen, a small window, and a floating mine. As can be seen in the drawing, he also included a key naming various parts of the submarine.

The *Nautilus* was refurbished and was moved to Brest, on France's Atlantic Coast, in the spring of 1801. There Fulton added a tank of compressed oxygen to increase the amount of time the submarine could stay underwater. He added a small window that provided enough light by which to operate the craft without using a candle. He also demonstrated a floating mine by blowing up a small sloop but found little support for it. By September his persistence had failed him. He returned to Paris with many excuses and a bold new plan to use submarines to plant mines in British harbors and the Thames River. Napoleon was excited by the scheme and sent word that he wished to see the *Nautilus*. Unfortunately Fulton had to report that he had taken apart the submarine because of its poor condition. In reality he was probably more concerned about its design being copied to build additional underwater vessels. He even refused to show the ship's drawings to government officials. Although this behavior could not possibly further his cause, it no longer mattered, because France and England made peace in October 1801.

The sudden end of hostilities must have brought mixed emotions to Fulton. There would be no further need for his submarine, which, in any event, had brought him neither fame nor fortune. Seldom at a loss for an idea to make money, Fulton began working on his next career, which was steamboats.

6. Steamboats
1802–1804

The first recorded attempt to power a ship with steam was in 1543. On June 13 of that year, Blasco de Garay, a Spanish naval officer under Charles V, propelled a ship of 200 tons (181 t) around the harbor of Barcelona, Spain, without oars or sails. Although de Garay did not provide details of the mechanism, witnesses reported that a steam engine with a copper boiler powered paddle wheels suspended over the side of the vessel. After the demonstration, de Garay apparently destroyed the mechanism after the government refused to provide protection and payment for his invention. Several other inventors tried to apply steam power to ships, especially after the steam engine came into widespread use in England during the eighteenth century. Of particular interest was a patent granted to Jonathan Hulls in 1736, for a steam-powered boat that used an engine built by Thomas Newcomen. The boat was to be used to tow sailing vessels in and out of harbors during calm periods. Around 1763, William Henry, keeper of the Juliana Library in Lancaster, Pennsylvania, built a

A description and a draft of Jonathan Hulls's steamboat from 1699 would appear on a 1737 pamphlet he published. The book and this rough drawing, which appears on the cover, give some idea of the machinery he proposed to make his steamboat run.

steamboat based on an engine he had seen in England. Although his first attempt sank in the Conestoga River, he built a second, which Robert Fulton may have seen while he lived in Lancaster.

After James Watt introduced the separate condenser in 1765, the number of steamboat experimenters increased. Among them were the Périer brothers in the mid-1770s and several Americans, particularly John Fitch and James Rumsey. Rumsey tested a steamboat on the Potomac River in the spring of 1786, several months after Fulton's stay at Warm Springs in Virginia, where Rumsey lived at the time. Rumsey made several trial runs from 1786 to 1788 using various boats and engines, none with particular success. He traveled to England in the summer of 1788, where he corresponded with Boulton and Watt before obtaining a patent in November of that year. Finding investors to build his ship, the *Columbian Maid*, proved difficult. Rumsey was forced to work in other fields to raise money, but in December 1792, his steamboat was ready for a trial run on the Thames. Unfortunately, before the trial run of his steamboat, Rumsey suffered a cerebral

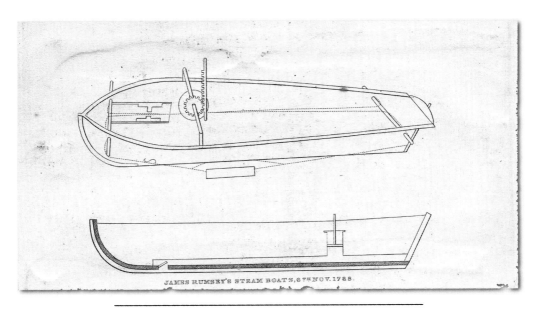

JAMES RUMSEY'S STEAM BOATS, 6TH NOV. 1788.

This is a drawing of James Rumsey's steamboat, the *Columbian Maid*, created on November 6, 1788. One can see where he planned to position the paddle wheel in the first drawing.

John Fitch is shown in the only known portrait of him ever published. It appeared in Lloyd's steamboat directory.

hemorrhage. The *Columbian Maid* made several successful runs on the Thames at a speed of 4 miles per hour (6 km/h), but without its prime mover, the project collapsed.

John Fitch invented his steamboat while in Pennsylvania in April 1785. He presented a model of a steamboat moved by chains, similar to a tank tread, to the American Philosophical Society in Philadelphia. Even before he had a working boat, Fitch obtained exclusive rights to employ steam navigation on the rivers of several states, including Virginia, New Jersey, Pennsylvania, Delaware, and New York. With these state grants, he was able to raise money to build a ship with oars driven by a steam engine. He demonstrated this ship to members of Congress at Philadelphia in August 1787. Fitch's second boat had three paddles in the rear. During the summer of 1790, Fitch operated regular passenger service with this boat on the Delaware River between Trenton and Philadelphia, reportedly losing money on every journey. During this time, Rumsey and Fitch engaged in nearly continuous litigation because of their respective steamboats. Fitch went to France to try his luck there but was unsuccessful.

Fitch's first steamboat is sailing on the Delaware River, opposite Philadelphia, in this 1856 picture by J. F. Reigart.

He returned to New York, where he experimented with a steam vessel using a screw propeller. Nearly broke, Fitch moved to Kentucky, where he died in 1798.

John Stevens of Hoboken, New Jersey, also had experimented with steamboats. His wife's brother, Robert R. Livingston, had designed a boat powered by horses plodding in a circle on the deck. Stevens advised him to use steam instead. Livingston's boat, named the *Polacca*, was completed and tested in late 1798. It moved briefly, but the engine was too heavy and shook excessively. The boat had to be abandoned. Livingston,

Robert Livingston (1746–1813) was an influential figure in his lifetime. He had been a member of the Continental Congress, was in charge of foreign affairs under the Articles of Confederation, and, in 1801, he was appointed foreign minister to France, where he negotiated the Louisiana Purchase. James Sharples created this portrait between 1795 and 1800.

chancellor of New York state, was undeterred and applied to take over the steam navigation monopoly granted to John Fitch in 1787. Because Fitch had not used his monopoly and was then living in Kentucky, the legislature agreed. They gave Livingston one year to build a boat that could travel from New York to Albany at 4 miles per hour (6 km/h). Livingston had many ideas, but in the end he had to rely on the more mechanically minded Stevens. Livingston and Stevens entered into a twenty-year contract in early 1800, to build and operate a steamboat on the Hudson.

Livingston, who had served in the Continental Congress in which he helped to draft the Declaration of Independence, served as the nation's first secretary of foreign affairs. In 1801, he was appointed by President Thomas Jefferson to be the American minister to France. In December 1801, he arrived in France to secure passage of U.S. ships on the Mississippi River past New Orleans. Perhaps inevitably, Livingston and Fulton were introduced and immediately realized their usefulness to each other. They shared a desire for great fame and fortune and began at once to work together to develop a successful steamboat.

They both realized a successful boat required a reliable steam engine. The British government restricted the export of steam engines to protect its industrial superiority and required a permit to be issued before an engine could be manufactured and sent to America. At that time, there were only six steam engines in America, so the policy seemed to work. Fulton's attempts to destroy the British fleet reduced his chances of receiving the required permit. Nevertheless he thought the effort to obtain a Watt engine was worthwhile, because this engine had been proven to work. Fulton could then focus his own efforts on improving the design of the ship and the propulsion mechanism.

Fulton's only experience in shipbuilding had been the *Nautilus*, but he had learned important principles from other naval architects, as well as from his own work studying canals and canal boats. He recognized that calculating the resistance of a vessel passing through the water was a complicated matter, involving not only the friction of the hull itself, but also the force necessary to push the water aside as the ship passed through it. His application of scientific principles to steam navigation made him unique among steamboat designers. More interested in getting the project done right than having it done quickly, Fulton hired Étienne Calla to build a model, which was ready in May 1802. He prepared a special testing basin, perhaps the first ever used, near the French resort town of Plombières, where Fulton was spending the summer. A spring-driven motor powered a pair of endless chains on each side of the boat to which paddles were attached. Fulton conducted a series of experiments in the testing basin to determine the best arrangement of the paddleboards.

This drawing is from the 1800s. It shows the *North River Steam Boat*, later called the *Clermont*. The circle in the center of the boat is the paddle wheel. The paddle was driven by steam. As the paddle turned through the water, it moved the boat forward.

Unlike most inventors, who worked in secret, Fulton welcomed the public to watch his experiments, both for their entertainment and for his own encouragement.

The experimental results convinced Fulton that his design was sound and would easily meet the 4-miles-per-hour (6-km/h) speed requirement of the New York monopoly. Most important, it would be profitable to operate. In October 1802, Fulton and Livingston agreed to become partners in an enterprise to build and to operate a steamboat that would run from New York to

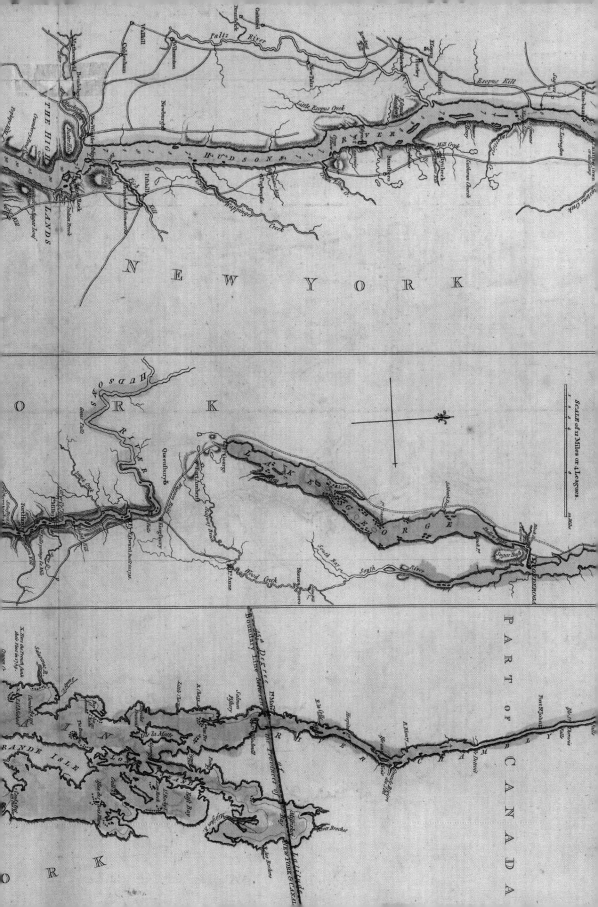

Albany on the Hudson River. The boat would not exceed 120 feet (36.5 m) in length and 8 feet (2.5 m) in width. It would run 8 miles per hour (13 km/h) in still water and carry at least sixty passengers. Fulton agreed to build a similar boat in Europe first and to obtain an American patent for the invention.

Attempts to borrow an engine from Boulton and Watt for the prototype boat failed. The Périer brothers had purchased a Watt engine for their waterworks in Paris and had built another for a steam-powered flour mill. Although their own earlier steamboat design had been unsuccessful, their work with Fulton on the *Nautilus* had given them great confidence in his engineering skills. They agreed to build the cylinder for the steam engine and to lend it to Fulton. Calla, the model maker, was hired to build the boiler and the moving parts for the engine. Fulton would design and build the boat itself. Although Fulton had been pleased with the paddles driven by endless chains on his first tests with the model boat, the full-size prototype had a pair of paddle wheels mounted on the side, a design that Fulton had tested after his return to Paris. He gave no reason for the change, but his careful experimentation must have confirmed the substitution.

Previous spread: Robert Fulton's *North River Steam Boat* would provide service between New York City and Albany. The Hudson River is shown in this map, published in 1777 in *The North American Atlas* by William Faden. The map shows the depths at various parts of the river.

Fulton also redesigned the hull to minimize the resistance of the water, using data from both French and English ship designers.

Fulton deposited a description and drawings of the boat in the French Conservatory of Arts and Trades early in 1803, in which he stated that the major purpose of the invention was to navigate the "long rivers of America" where roads did not exist or were unsuitable for hauling freight. Surprisingly he did not mention the Hudson River. Instead he referred to the Mississippi River, by which most commercial goods were reaching the interior of America. He might have known from his partner, Livingston, that negotiations were underway with Napoléon to sell Louisiana to the United States, thereby securing the entire Mississippi River for the United States.

The prototype steamboat progressed well under the expert supervision of Calla and Périer. The ship was built in public view next to Périer's waterworks on the Seine and attracted a lot of attention due to its unusual appearance. The first trials were delayed when the ship was damaged, likely at the hands of bargemen afraid of competition from the strange craft. The steam machinery was saved and installed on a new boat, which was 74 feet (22.5 m) long and 8 feet (2 m) wide. The boat was tested in late July or early August 1803, and a public trial was held on August 9 before enormous crowds.

Smoke billowed from the boat's stack as Fulton guided it into the Seine. He towed two boats up and down the river without difficulty and demonstrated the maneuverability provided by the side-mounted paddle wheels. The demonstration was a complete success. Despite the success, Fulton had probably worn out his welcome in France. He had offered his steamboats to Napoléon earlier that year, but the French dictator was tired of imaginary projects. He considered Fulton a charlatan and an imposter. He told his advisers "not to speak of him again." Fulton was crushed, although he should not have been surprised by this reaction from the first consul.

Confident of his future success in America, Fulton ordered an engine from Boulton and Watt to be delivered to one of Livingston's cousins in New York City. He also assured them that he would get the necessary export permit from the British government. In October the firm replied that they had not received the permit and could not fulfill the contract. Telling his partner and friends that he had to stop in England to finalize the contract before proceeding to America, Fulton settled his account and left France in April 1804. Despite his waiting friends in America, his business in England would occupy him for more than two years.

7. Torpedoes 1804–1806

War had resumed between Britain and France in May 1803. The Napoleonic Wars, as the conflict is now called, would span an immense area of the globe and would last for twelve years. Both Moscow and Washington would be captured and burned before the conflict ended. In 1803, the troops of Napoléon's Grande Armée massed on the Channel coast, making preparations to invade England. The English Channel is so narrow that English villagers could see the fires of the French troops. According to the first consul, France needed to control the English Channel for six hours to allow his army to cross the 20 miles (32 km) to England. The only obstacle to Napoléon's plan was the British navy, which was skilled and powerful but alone, because Great Britain had no allies. The British knew that the balance of naval power could be instantly upset by technological innovation, particularly if it were employed with skill and surprise. The inventions of Robert Fulton fell into this category. The British decided that having Fulton on their side of the conflict

This battle scene created in 1798 by Pellerin depicts a battle from the Napoleonic Wars that occurred on July 13, 1798, in Egypt. Napoléon called it the Battle of the Pyramids, but it actually did not take place anywhere near them. His victory here was short-lived. On August 1, 1798, Napoléon's army would suffer a huge defeat at the hands of Horatio Nelson at the Battle of the Nile.

would be much more comforting than would be the potential of his assisting the French.

Sometime in 1803, an agent of the British secret service approached Fulton with a proposal. The agent told Fulton that Great Britain would pay him well for the use of his naval technology. Fulton named his price. The following March, the agent returned, offering less money and a letter guaranteeing "utmost liberality and generosity" for Fulton should he choose to help England. Fulton accepted and arrived in England in May 1804 to defend the fleet he had not long before offered to destroy. Fulton's actions seem worse to us than they were in his day. Throughout the seventeenth and eighteenth centuries, numerous and even distinguished soldiers offered their services to the highest bidder, a practice that only slowly waned through time as nationalism and patriotism became more popular. That said, the simple fact is that Napoléon had rejected Fulton's devices, and the British were willing to pay for them.

Fulton, using the pseudonym Robert Francis (which seems to have fooled no one), negotiated with the British government. At first this went no better than negotiations with the French. A commission was

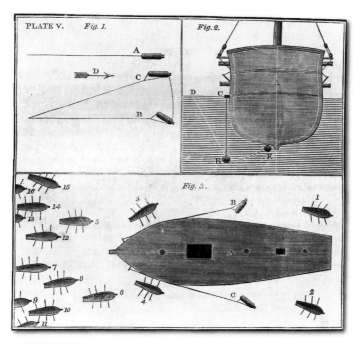

These are some of Fulton's sketches (Plate V) of torpedoes from his 1810 book, *Torpedo War and Submarine Explosions*. The torpedoes are meant to be attached to enemy ships, which are indicated by the shapes with the six lines extending out of them.

appointed to review Fulton's submarine and bombs, and they recommended pursuing the bombs, which literally promised more bang for the buck, as we might say today. While government officials were considering Fulton's proposal, they granted him a permit to build and to export a steam engine. Fulton traveled to the Boulton and Watt factory in Birmingham, England, to work out the final details. The government suddenly agreed to pay Fulton even more than he had demanded for his weapons, raising his suspicions that its real motive was to control him and the invention, not necessarily to employ them in battle. Nevertheless the agreement was signed in July 1804, and Fulton began work on his torpedoes, which today we would call mines. Each one weighed up to 2 tons (2 t) and was designed primarily to destroy enemy ships, although it could also be effective against coastal fortifications. The torpedoes would be carried to the vicinity of enemy ships by small craft rowed by volunteer sailors under the cover of darkness.

The first attack took place on October 2, 1804, against French ships in Boulogne Harbor. Several of the torpedoes exploded, causing great confusion but little damage. The attack raised a storm of protest from naval officers who considered this kind of action to be more akin to burglary than to warfare. The government, however, seemed pleased with the possibilities, and another attack took place in Boulogne in December. Like the first, it delivered few results. The British admiralty apparently tired of the project and essentially placed the enterprise on hold in hopes that it would wither and die. Fulton, unsurprisingly, felt that the true potential of the torpedoes had not been fairly demonstrated, and he wrote to the prime minister to state his position. Robert Fulton's letter

British leader Robert Stewart, second marquis of Londonderry, was known generally as Viscount Castlereagh. He lived between 1769 and 1822.

was forwarded to Viscount Castlereagh, war secretary, who was quite attracted to Robert Fulton's proposal. Castlereagh proposed to use the torpedoes in conjunction with Sir William Congreve's new rockets. Congreve's rockets became famous a decade later in the British attack on Fort McHenry in Baltimore, Maryland, where "the

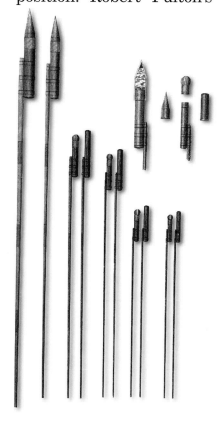

These sketches of Sir William Congreve's rockets were created for his book, *A Concise Account of the Origin and Progress of the Rocket System.*

Francis Scott Key is shown observing Fort McHenry from aboard ship. Britain was unable to defeat the fort in 1814.

War broke out in 1812 over Britain's attempts to control American shipping and other activities. When the British fleet kidnapped an elderly American physician, Francis Scott Key was sent to negotiate for his release. The British fleet placed Key under guard while they carried out an attack against Baltimore. On September 13, 1814, the British attacked Baltimore by land and by sea. The next morning, Key saw the American flag still flying at Fort McHenry. The Baltimore fort had not been defeated! Overjoyed, Key wrote the poem "Defence of Fort McHenry," which later became known as "The Star-Spangled Banner." It became America's national anthem in 1931.

rockets' red glare, the bombs bursting in air" inspired Francis Scott Key to write the poem that became a song and the national anthem of the United States.

Castlereagh's attack in Boulogne Harbor was not carried out until September 30, 1805, but Fulton was only a spectator, and the torpedoes were again a dismal failure. Desperate to demonstrate the military value of the torpedo, he was allowed to do so with the captured Danish brig *Dorothea*. Planning the October 15 demonstration carefully, Fulton orchestrated an attack with a 170-pound (77-kg) torpedo, carried into position by a small boat. The torpedo found its mark, and the ship was utterly destroyed, becoming a "black mass floating on the surface." Fulton and the other observers were stunned by the force of the explosion, which would have instantly killed anyone on the vessel. Castlereagh paid Fulton a large reward for the demonstration, which Fulton promptly shared with his sisters and brother back in Pennsylvania. Castlereagh ordered a further attack on Boulogne in late October, with little result due to the onset of poor weather. Castlereagh decided to send Fulton and Congreve with their weapons to Admiral Nelson's fleet at Cádiz, Spain.

Nelson spoiled their plan, however, by defeating the combined French and Spanish fleets at Cape Trafalgar on October 21, 1805. This was one of the greatest British naval victories. Admiral Nelson died

This document shows a bird's-eye view of the October 1805 Battle of Trafalgar. This nineteenth-century print is held at the Biblioteca Nacional (the National Library) in Madrid, Spain.

in this battle. The threat of invasion instantly vanished, and with it the necessity for Fulton and his inventions. His salary was halted. For the next year he pestered the British government with letters and threats, but he was only able to obtain a small additional payment toward the sums promised him in 1804. His work in Europe done, Fulton sailed home to America, arriving in New York Harbor on December 13, 1806, nearly twenty years after he had left Philadelphia. Waiting for him in a New York warehouse was a Boulton and Watt steam engine.

8. Pioneer 1806–1807

More than fifteen years had passed since John Fitch had operated his short-lived steamboat service on the Delaware River. Several other inventors in America had tried to build steamboats, but without success. The technical and financial obstacles to building and operating a steamboat were significant. There were only six steam engines in America in 1803, providing limited experience in building these boats. Any potential steamboat operator also faced significant legal obstacles, because many states had already granted exclusive rights for steamboat service to individuals who were unable to provide it. Existing patents provided another impediment, for these covered many of the basic fundamentals of steamboat design. Just as "the heavy hand of Watt" had kept many useful steam-engine improvements from reaching the commercial market until his patents expired, the combination of federal patents on inventions and exclusive state grants to use waterways for navigation made any successful steamboat service very difficult to achieve. John Fitch had received a fourteen-year grant to run steamboats on the waterways of New York state in 1787, but had never done so. Robert Livingston was able to take over this monopoly just before he went to France. Livingston also had signed a twenty-year agreement with his brother-in-law, John Stevens, to build and operate a steamboat between New York City and Albany on the Hudson River. While Livingston was in Europe, Stevens built and tested the *Little Juliana*, a 68-foot (21-m) steamboat powered by twin screw propellers. It never entered com-

The engine used in *Little Juliana* can be viewed at the Smithsonian Institution in Washington, D.C.

mercial service but today its engine is on display in the Smithsonian Institution in Washington, D.C., as the oldest American steam engine in existence. Livingston, meanwhile, had returned from Europe in June 1805, and had retired to Clermont, his estate on the Hudson River south of Albany.

Next page: This is Clermont Manor as it stands today.
Inset: This is a view of the Hudson River from Clermont Manor.

After Fulton returned from England in December 1806, he wrote to his partner, Livingston. Instead of meeting with him, however, Fulton traveled to Philadelphia to visit the Barlows, the friends he had lived with in Europe. He also wrote to President Thomas Jefferson, requesting that government agents record the water velocity and depth at various points along the Mississippi River for each month of the year. Fulton also obtained information on the currents and the river traffic through New Orleans. This allowed him to calculate potential profits from a steamboat service on the Mississippi River, which must have made service for the short, 150-mile (241-km) journey from New York to Albany seem unimportant. Then Fulton went to Washington and met with William Thornton, a physician and architect who was in charge of the federal patent office.

Fulton then visited Lancaster to call on the surveyor Andrew Ellicott, who had also measured the currents of the Mississippi River. Fulton also might have visited his siblings and his mother's grave before traveling to Philadelphia, where a letter from Livingston awaited him. Fulton's partner was very irritated with Fulton's interest in navigation on the Mississippi River because the original purpose of their agreement, steam service on the Hudson, remained undone. Fulton's interest in the Mississippi River was understandable, because the Louisiana Purchase, which had been negotiated by

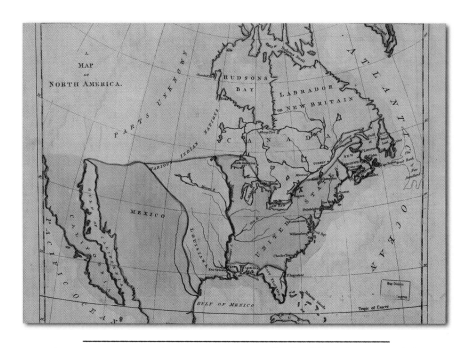

The Louisiana Purchase in 1803 nearly doubled the size of the United States as visible in this May 1, 1803, map by J. Luffman engraved for Luffman's *Geographical Principles*.

Livingston while Livingston was in Paris, had opened up enormous lands in the West that would require an entire new transportation network. Public interest in Louisiana was also high, because Meriwether Lewis and William Clark had just returned from an expedition to the new territory with tales of its splendor.

Fulton traveled to Clermont to meet with Livingston for the first time in nearly three years. The Clermont estate had been established in 1728, by Livingston's father. The estate comprised the southern third of what is now Columbia County and was the second-largest private landholding in colonial New York. It had been burned by the British during the American Revolution, after which Livingston built a new house to match the beauty of the original. In 1909, it was also destroyed by fire. Today a small portion of the original estate is owned by New York state and is a national historic landmark.

The two men agreed to proceed with the Hudson River steamboat, and Fulton returned to New York to start construction. He hired Charles Browne, a shipbuilder on the East River, to build a boat 146 feet (44.5 m) long and

The HMS *Leopard* attacked the USS *Chesapeake* on June 21, 1807. This watercolor on paper is attributed to Irwin Bevan (1852–1940), a Welsh-born naval historian. Accounts that went with Bevan's paintings relied heavily on detailed contemporary accounts of the military actions between the United States and Great Britain that were written down in letters, reports, and newspapers.

12 feet (4 m) wide with an interior height of 6 ½ feet (2 m), tall enough for "a man with a hat on." Browne promised to deliver it in eight weeks. Fulton picked up the steam engine from the warehouse and hired other workmen to fabricate the paddle wheels and the boiler.

While the ship was under construction, the British warship HMS *Leopard* attacked the USS *Chesapeake* off Cape Henry. In the attack, three American sailors were killed, eighteen were wounded, and four were kidnapped. Fulton had offered his torpedoes and submarine to the American navy earlier, and, after the attack, he was given permission to demonstrate his bombs in New York Harbor. The devices did not explode at first, and much of the crowd left before Fulton repaired the mechanism and blew up a derelict brig. In the meantime, President Jefferson asked Fulton to assist in building the defenses of New Orleans by surveying a canal between the Mississippi River and Lake Pontchartrain, near New Orleans, but Fulton politely refused.

Four years to the day after demonstrating his steamboat on the Seine, Fulton fired up the boiler on the new vessel and ran it 1 mile (1.6 km) or so down the East River, easily outrunning all the sloops on the water. A week later, Fulton moved the ship to the North River, as the section of the Hudson River along Manhattan was then called. Several of Livingston's friends took the short journey, including a U.S. senator. The following

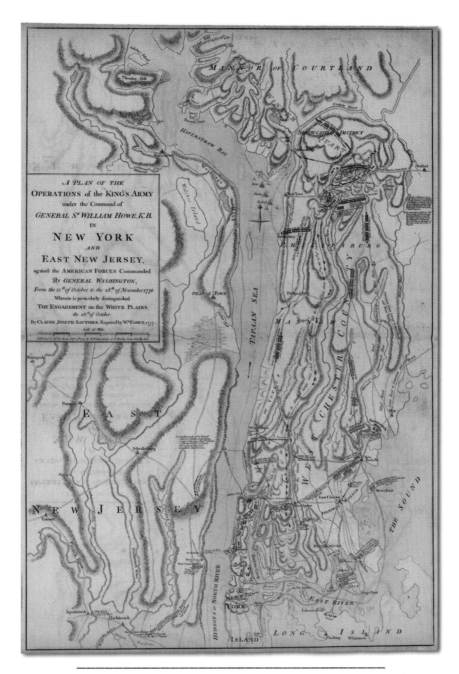

Fulton's steamboat service ran along the North River, which is clearly visible in this 1777 map by William Faden.

day, Monday, August 17, 1807, Fulton and a skeleton crew set out for Albany, 150 miles (241 km) to the north. They sailed at 1:00 P.M. and arrived at the Clermont landing, 110 miles (177 km) to the north, exactly twenty-four hours later, achieving a speed of 4 ½ miles per hour (7 km/h). On August 19, the ship sailed the remaining 40 miles (64 km) to Albany, arriving just after 5:00 P.M. The following morning, Fulton hung a sign advertising steamboat service to New York City starting the following day. The fare was seven dollars. Only two brave French passengers made the journey. After a one-hour layover at Clermont to drop off Livingston and his guests, the boat continued the journey down the Hudson, arriving in New York at 4:00 P.M. on Friday. Exhausted and ecstatic, Fulton had finally achieved the success that had so long eluded him. Remaining successful would prove far more difficult.

9. Entrepreneur
1807–1815

Fulton's steamboat began regular passenger service on September 4, 1807, leaving New York at 6:00 P.M. and arriving in Albany thirty-six hours later. Fulton registered the boat as the *North River Steam Boat*. Only after his death did the ship become known as the *Clermont*. For some time, the word "steamboat" was enough to distinguish it from every other vessel in the world.

The rest of the season went well except for a few minor collisions with sloops, whose captains were not used to the strange vessel that defied wind and tide. Some of these collisions may not have been accidental, as the steamboat was competition for sailing vessels on the same route. Despite his boat's success, Fulton considered it to be mostly experimental. He

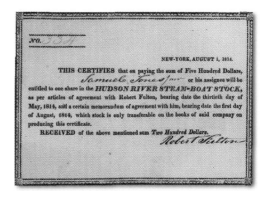

This is a stock certificate for the Hudson River steamboat, called the *North River Steam Boat*. It was made out to Samuel Jones Jr. in August 1814 and signed by Robert Fulton.

recommended that it be rebuilt with a new, wider hull and more luxurious fittings. Livingston thought that two more moderate boats would be more practical, but Fulton prevailed and had the ship rebuilt during the winter. The ship was then 149 feet (45 m) long, and its wider hull had twice the volume of the original craft, allowing it to carry more passengers and cargo.

The second season of service began on April 26, 1808. Two weeks before, the New York legislature had granted Fulton and Livingston exclusive rights to operate steamboats on the river, allowing five years for each boat, up to a maximum of thirty years. Coal had been used for the initial round-trip to Albany, but it was not reliably available. Wood was used as a fuel thereafter, requiring more volume for storage but producing less smoke. Nevertheless passengers complained about the smoke as well as the noise, the overheated cabins, and the poor service at the landing places. Yet they flocked aboard the boat, which provided reliable and generally punctual service. A single trip in July carried one hundred and forty passengers. The boat was making a good profit for its owners.

The significantly reduced travel time might have been enough in itself to attract passengers, but Fulton wanted to provide quality service as well as excellent accommodations, which were generally lacking in the competing sailing vessels. He was forced to make an extensive list of rules governing conduct on board the ship. Smoking was limited to certain areas, card playing was banned after 10:00 P.M. in the ladies' cabin, and lying down was forbidden while wearing boots and shoes. Passengers who broke the rules had to pay a fine, which was used to buy wine for the other passengers. Fulton's careful planning and supervision, aided by his hiring competent and able crewmen, delivered extraordinary success.

In addition to the steamboat enterprise, Fulton was engaged in a wide range of other activities. Despite the profits to be made in steam navigation, his major passion was perfecting his naval weaponry and selling it to the American government, which faced grave dangers from the powerful British navy. President Jefferson had convinced Congress to pass the Embargo Act in December 1807, forbidding trade with the British. This appeared to have no effect on the British but virtually ruined American commerce, particularly in seaports such as New York, which was deserted. Fulton also found time to write a short but thorough report on the advantages of canals, which was included in Secretary of the Treasury Albert Gallatin's *Report on Public Roads and Canals*, published in April 1808. Fulton once again pointed out the advantages of building a canal across Pennsylvania, including, among other factors, the significant increase in value of lands near the canal, but the report appears to have received little attention in that state. It was, however, read avidly in New York, where the state legislature had just

Rembrandt Peale painted this portrait of Albert Gallatin in 1805.
Gallatin was a very important figure in U.S. history. He served as
secretary of the treasury for many years. He was a founder of the
American Ethnological Society, making valuable contributions on
languages of the Native Americans. He also served as president
of the New-York Historical Society in the mid-1800s.

approved the survey of a canal to connect Lake Erie with the Hudson River at Albany.

A month after sending his canal report to Gallatin, 42-year-old Fulton was married to 24-year-old Harriet Livingston, a relative of his steamboat partner. Her father had died when she was fourteen, but she lived comfortably in a house on the original Livingston estate. Unlike most of her female relatives, she had received a good education in a boarding school, and she was drawn to the talented and intelligent Fulton.

The same day that Fulton was married, John Stevens signed a contract for a 100-foot-long (30-m-long) steamboat that he named the *Phoenix*. It would run between Hoboken and Albany in defiance of the Livingston-Fulton monopoly. Stevens wrote to Fulton suggesting that their efforts could somehow be joined together, but Fulton was noncommittal. Livingston was irritated and sent his brother-in-law a long defense of his exclusive right to use steamboats on the waters of New York State. He suggested that Stevens could operate his boat between New York City and New Brunswick, New Jersey, and from Philadelphia to Trenton, New Jersey, on the Delaware, as long as Stevens acknowledged that he was operating with permission from Livingston and Fulton. Stevens refused this offer, and because his original agreement with Livingston was still in force, he had a strong legal claim to a share of the *North River Steam Boat*'s profits. Despite their strained business and legal relationship, Fulton welcomed Stevens to view the remodeled ship and to share technical ideas. Stevens tested the *Phoenix* in July 1808, and the boat made a speed of 5 ½ miles per hour (9 km/h), but the higher-pressure boiler proved unsatisfactory and required significant modifications. In the meantime, Livingston and Fulton had engaged Livingston's brother John to establish steamboat service from New York City to Staten Island and New Jersey. They had a steamboat built for this, which was named the *Raritan*. Fulton and Livingston also ordered a second boat for their Hudson River service. Named the *Car of Neptune*, it was to be even larger and more luxurious than the remodeled *North River Steam Boat*. Fulton's first child was also born that year, in October, and was named Robert Barlow Fulton for Joel Barlow, with whom Fulton and Harriet were now living in Washington, D.C.

After the second successful season of the *North River Steam Boat*'s operation, Fulton applied for and received a federal patent that gave him exclusive rights to his invention for fourteen years. Fulton then returned to promoting submarine warfare. President Jefferson was able to provide Fulton with funds to conduct further experiments. Fulton demonstrated a harpoon gun to Jefferson, President-elect James Madison, and several members of Congress in February 1809, and took the occasion to seek support for his torpedoes for use in mining enemy harbors. The response was cool, however, so he wrote to his friend the French minister of finance and

This hand-colored map by John Mitchell (1711–1768) shows the east coast of New Jersey and New York. John Livingston's steamboat service ferried passengers between New York City, colored red, and Staten Island, colored blue.

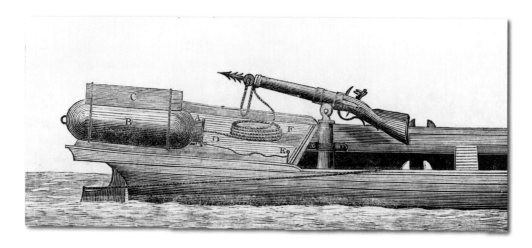

Robert Fulton created this drawing of a harpoon gun
coming from the top of a submarine. It was published as
Plate IV in his 1810 book *Torpedo War and Submarine Explosions*.
Notice the barbed tip of the harpoon. These barbs would
catch inside the target and make it difficult to remove.

offered to "sweep the British fleet from the Channel,"
perhaps forgetting that France was as much an enemy of
American interests as was Britain. France had not been
particularly friendly toward America after America had
refused to help in France's war with Britain.

Fulton and Harriet set up a household in New York
on Chambers Street, just north of City Hall, where pigs
and cows still roamed the streets. The *North River
Steam Boat* began its third season of operation in
March 1809. Fulton and Livingston agreed to begin

steamboat operations between New Orleans and Natchez, Louisiana, on the Mississippi River, a 300-mile (483-km) run with relatively deep water. Never one to make small plans, Fulton also wrote to the Bavarian government offering to organize and operate a steamboat line on the Danube River.

The *Phoenix* began passenger service between New York City and New Brunswick, New Jersey, but John Livingston threatened to provide direct competing service at a lower cost with the *Raritan*. Stevens chose to avoid direct confrontation with his competitors and sailed the *Phoenix* to Philadelphia in June 1809. He planned to operate passenger service on the Delaware River between Philadelphia and Bordentown in neighboring New Jersey, the same route that John Fitch had served in 1790. The 240-mile (386-km) journey was the first by a steamboat on the open sea. It took almost two weeks and was a remarkable achievement. Shortly thereafter the *Phoenix* began regular passenger service, with entertainment provided to attract passengers. The *Phoenix* proved difficult to handle, reflecting its mechanical imperfections. In December Stevens finally compromised with Fulton and Livingston and agreed to share all present and future patent rights regarding steamboats. On the Hudson River, the *Car of Neptune* began service in August 1809.

Despite the ongoing success of the steamboat, or perhaps because of it, Fulton devoted much of 1810 to submarine warfare. His sixty-page pamphlet on the subject, *Torpedo War and Submarine Explosions*, was published early that year. He aggressively lobbied government officials for funds to put on another demonstration. In March 1810, he received the funds with the condition that a demonstration be concluded before the end of the year. Finally receiving exactly what he had wished for (in fact more, for Congress gave him twice the sum he had requested), Fulton spent the next several months furiously preparing his devices, distracted only briefly by the birth of his daughter Juliet. Unfortunately the demonstrations were largely unsuccessful. Despite an unfavorable recommendation by a committee appointed to oversee his work, war with Britain seemed unavoidable, and the largely unprepared government saw no reason not to allow Fulton to continue his work.

Quite naturally the commercial success of Fulton's steamboat enterprise attracted competitors. The *Vermont*, a copy of the *North River Steam Boat* built by one of Fulton's former workmen, was launched on Lake Champlain in 1808, and it began passenger service in July 1809. Another competitor planned service on the Delaware alongside the *Phoenix*. Only the proposed service on the Mississippi River seemed secure from competition. Fulton hired Nicholas Roosevelt to build a boat in Pittsburgh to begin service on the Mississippi River. Fulton applied for and received an improved steamboat patent in February 1811. This did not prevent the appearance of a competing steamboat on the Hudson River in April, financed by a group of Albany investors. This ship, named the *Hope*, was also a clone of the *North River Steam Boat*, much to Fulton's annoyance. A second ship, the *Perseverance*, was run by the same investors and began operating in early September. Fulton and Livingston sought an injunction against the Albany group in early August, but the judge refused to grant it. The two men then filed suit against their Albany competitors. They asked the court to honor the terms of their grant by forfeiting the *Hope* to them, as allowed by law. An injunction was again denied, forcing an appeal that was not heard until March 1812.

Despite the appearance of competition, the two ships operated by Fulton and Livingston continued to deliver strong profits. Fulton began work on a new ship, the *Paragon*, 170 feet (52 m) long by 28 feet (8.5 m) wide and designed from the keel up to be a floating palace. Meanwhile Nicholas Roosevelt continued work on the *New Orleans* in Pittsburgh. Unlike the *North River Steam Boat*, which had a paddle wheel on each side of the hull, the *New Orleans* was driven by a single wheel in the stern. Fulton and Livingston obtained exclusive rights to use steamboats on the Mississippi River. The *New Orleans* began its 2,000-mile (3,219-km) journey down the Ohio and Mississippi Rivers on September 27, 1811, but could not navigate the rapids

This is a re-creation of riverboat *New Orleans* from 1909. *New Orleans* was the first steamboat to navigate the Ohio and Mississippi Rivers in 1811. It was designed with the paddle on its stern.

downstream of Louisville until late in November. The boat did not arrive in New Orleans until January 12, 1812. During its trip, it also endured the New Madrid earthquakes of the previous month, the most powerful ever recorded in North America.

The safe arrival of the *New Orleans* was good news for Fulton and Livingston. Shortly afterward a court in Albany granted an injunction suspending service by the *Hope* and the *Perseverance*. Fulton was soon busy on two new boats, the *Jersey* and the *Firefly*. The *Firefly* was a smaller version of the *North River Steam Boat*, but the *Jersey* was a unique design—a twin-hulled catamaran on which the steam engine drove a single paddle wheel suspended between the two hulls. One hull was set up for passengers and the other for cargo, horses, and livestock. Designed for ferry service across the Hudson River, the *Jersey* did not need to turn around after each trip. It reversed the waterwheel for the return journey.

This was a particularly busy time in Fulton's life. His second daughter, Cornelia, was born in August 1812. A month later, a compromise was reached with the Albany competitors that resulted in Fulton's purchase of the *Hope* while Aaron Ogden secured an interest in the *Perseverance*.

Robert R. Livingston died from a stroke in February 1813, leaving his estate and his finances in dreadful condition. Within hours of hearing this distressing news, Fulton received a second blow when he learned that his close friend Joel Barlow had died in December. Barlow had been appointed American minister to France and had died while on a diplomatic mission in Poland. After Livingston's death, Fulton was running an enormous and far-flung enterprise virtually by himself. The War of 1812 with Great Britain had begun, and British ships were blockading American harbors. Several of Fulton's torpedoes were used to attack these British ships, with the most success coming from a near miss that severely shook the HMS *Plantagenet* at the mouth of Chesapeake Bay. Fulton designed an underwater cannon that did well in tests but was not adopted. He also drew up plans for a steam-powered warship as well as an iron-plated vessel, which he called the *Mute*.

Fulton began several new enterprises early in 1814, including a scheme to supply coal to New York City. Fulton had used coal for the first voyage of the *North River Steam Boat*, but he had changed to wood because enough coal was not available. Wood itself became scarce as the demand for firewood increased. Meanwhile the British blockade cut off coal deliveries from Liverpool and Virginia. Fulton proposed mining coal on land he had purchased along the Mississippi River and taking it by barge to New Orleans, where it would be loaded onto ships for delivery to New York. His land proved to have no coal, and the enterprise was abandoned.

A second project was the Erie Canal, which had been under consideration for several years to connect the Hudson River and Lake Erie in New York. Both Fulton and Livingston had been appointed to the Erie Canal Commission in 1811. In 1814, Fulton and Gouverneur Morris, the president of the commission, published a pamphlet promoting the construction of the canal. The promoters of the Erie Canal had been criticized for not taking advantage of Lake Ontario as a trade route, but British control of that lake during the War of 1812 silenced those arguments. Because of the war and numerous other reasons, construction of the Erie Canal did not start until 1817.

Fulton's third endeavor in 1814 was a steam-powered warship. It was approved in July 1814. One month later, the British landed on the shores of the Pautuxent River in Maryland. They marched overland to the federal capital in Washington, where they burned every government building except William Thornton's patent office. Thornton successfully defended the office by arguing that it contained private property. Fulton's steam warship was launched in October 1814, several weeks after Congreve's rockets had lit up the sky over Fort McHenry in Baltimore. Fulton's warship was christened *Fulton I,* a tribute to its inventor. Fulton continued to work on it even as he took part in a particularly bitter legal battle with Aaron Ogden over rights to use steamboats on New Jersey waters. Exhausted from his many labors, Fulton fell ill with pneumonia and died on February 23, 1815, at the age of forty-nine. He was buried with great honors in the Livingston family plot at Trinity Church in New York City.

Fulton's mother had died while he was in Europe, and his youngest sister, Polly, died shortly before his own death in 1815. His widow, Harriet, remarried two years after his death and died in 1826. His son, Robert, never married, but his daughters did and produced nine Fulton grandchildren. Money owed to Fulton by

This is the headstone on Robert Fulton's tomb at Trinity Church in New York City.

the U.S. government for work he had done prior to his death was not paid until 1847.

The *Fulton I* was not yet completed when the War of 1812 ended. Despite this she was finished in order to test the concept of a steam warship. Later she became a barracks ship before she was accidentally blown up in 1829, when a careless guard carried a lighted candle into the gunpowder magazine. The navy did not build a second steam vessel until 1837, which it christened the *Fulton II*.

Steam power was widely used by the American navy during the Civil War. Underwater torpedoes, or mines, are still widely used by navies throughout the world. The Confederacy used several submarines during the American Civil War. The Confederate ship *Hunley* became the first submarine to sink an enemy ship, although the vessel itself sank after the attack, killing all aboard. The terrible effect of submarines was first demonstrated in World War I (1914–1918), drawing widespread criticism along with numerous imitators.

The Erie Canal in New York opened in 1825, and it was the most successful canal built in America. Boats passed from Buffalo to Albany on the canal, where steamboats then carried the cargo to New York City. As Fulton had predicted in his 1796 treatise, the land along the canal became very valuable and the Erie Canal made New York City the most important seaport and financial center in the country. As the duke of Bridgewater's canal began a series of canal building in England, the Erie Canal began an era of canal building in America. The Erie Canal proved the most successful and enduring small canal. Heavy machinery developed later in the nineteenth century made much larger canals possible, including those in Suez, Panama, and Saint Lawrence. These canals carry oceangoing ships. Fulton's plan to supply coal to New York City was unsuccessful, but he was correct in predicting its widespread use. Coal replaced wood as the primary energy source in America during the nineteenth century.

The steamboat is clearly Robert Fulton's greatest legacy. Despite the work of numerous inventors, the steamboat was only a curiosity until Fulton sailed from New York City to Albany in August 1807. By 1826, there were sixteen steamboats operating in the United States and more than one hundred by 1840. More than six hundred steamboats operated on western rivers by 1850, increasing to more than eight hundred by 1860.

Many later steamboats used high-pressure steam boilers and engines, which were very dangerous. Despite the rudimentary nature of steam engineering in Fulton's day, no passenger was killed or seriously injured on a Fulton boat during his lifetime, which is a remarkable record. The U.S. Supreme Court ruled in 1824 that the federal government controlled navigation on rivers, striking down the various state monopolies that had been granted.

Before Robert Fulton built his steamboat, workable steamboats were virtually nonexistent in America. By the 1860s, there were more than 800 steamboats in operation. *Mary Powell* was painted by James Bard in 1861.

Robert Fulton was both a visionary and an opportunist. He had no lack of courage, evidenced by his attacking warships in a fragile submarine. Unlike many other inventors, Fulton willingly shared his ideas and his concepts with others. He likewise borrowed ideas heavily from others, which he sometimes admitted and sometimes didn't. He was most perceptive in grasping that technology by itself was of little value. Merely inventing or demonstrating a machine was not enough, it had to be made useful, productive, and, most important, profitable. Later inventors, such as Thomas Edison, Henry Ford, and Bill Gates, learned this lesson as well.

Timeline

1763–1767	James Watt invents a separate condenser for the steam engine.
1765	Robert Fulton is born.
1775–1783	The American Revolution is fought.
1776	David Bushnell attacks British warships with his submarine the *Turtle*.
1779	Fulton is apprenticed as a silversmith.
1787	John Fitch receives a monopoly to operate steamboats in New York.
1787	Fulton sails to London to study art.
1789	On July 14, the French Revolution begins.
1794	Fulton wins a silver medal for his marble cutting machine.
1796	Fulton publishes *A Treatise on the Improvement of Canal Navigation*.
1797	In June, Fulton travels to France.
	In December, Fulton offers a submarine

proposal to the French government.

1798   In March, Robert R. Livingston takes over Fitch's steamboat monopoly.

1800   Fulton opens a panorama in Paris.

On June 13, Fulton demonstrates his submarine the *Nautilus* on the Seine River in Paris.

The *Nautilus* attacks British warships.

1802   On October 10, Fulton and Livingston become partners.

1803   In April, the United States buys the Louisiana Territory from France.

In May, the Napoleonic Wars begin between England and France.

On August 9, Fulton demonstrates a steamboat on the Seine River.

1804   In the spring, Fulton moves to England.

1804–1805 Fulton's torpedoes are used in attacks on French ships at Boulogne.

1806   In December, Fulton returns to America.

1807   On August 17, Fulton's steamboat

begins its journey from New York City to Albany.

On September 4, Fulton's *North River Steam Boat* begins steamboat service between New York City and Albany.

1808	Fulton marries Harriet Livingston.
1809	In February, Fulton receives a patent for his steamboat.
1810	Fulton publishes *Torpedo War and Submarine Explosions*.
1811	In February, Fulton receives a second patent for his steamboat.

Fulton's steamboat the *New Orleans* begins to travel to New Orleans.

1812	On June 19, the War of 1812 begins.
1813	In February, Robert Livingston dies.
1814	Congress approves funds for Fulton to build steam warships.

In October, the first steam warship, *Fulton I*, is launched in New York City.

1815	On February 23, Fulton dies.

Glossary

accumulated (uh-KYOO-myuh-layt-ed) To have gathered or collected, often in gradual degrees.

admiralty (AD-muh-ruhl-tee) The officials or the department of state having charge of naval affairs, as in Great Britain.

annihilate (uh-NY-uh-layt) To reduce to utter ruin or nonexistence; destroy utterly.

apprentice (uh-PREN-tis) A person learning a trade or craft from a skilled worker.

aqueduct (A-kweh-duhkt) A bridgelike structure that carries water or a canal across a valley or over a river.

artisans (AR-tih-zuhnz) People skilled in applied arts; craftspeople. Silversmiths and carpenters are artisans.

cerebral hemorrage (seh-REE-bral HEHM-rij) Leakage of blood from a blood vessel into the brain, often followed by brain damage; a type of stroke.

charlatan (SHAR-luh-tin) A fraud or faker; one who pretends to have knowledge that one does not possess.

civic (SIH-vik) Pertaining to citizenship; or civic duties.

commissions (kuh-MIH-shenz) Gives an order for.

destitute (DES-tih-toot) Lacking food, clothing, and shelter.

dexterity (dek-STER-eh-tee) Skill in using the hands or body.

diligently (DIH-leh-jent-lee) Constantly working to accomplish something.

Embargo Act (im-BAR-goh AKT) The Embargo Act of 1807, passed on December 22, 1807, which forbade all international trade to and from American ports.

fabricate (FA-brih-kayt) To make by art, skill, and labor. To construct.

Hessian (HEH-shen) A German mercenary from Hesse hired by England during the American Revolution.

impediment (im-PEH-deh-ment) Obstruction; hindrance; obstacle.

indenture (in-DEHN-chur) A contract by which a person, as an apprentice, is bound to service.

injunction (in-JUHNK-shun) A court order requiring the person or persons to whom it is directed to do a particular act or to refrain from doing a particular act.

insatiable (in-SAY-sheh-bul) Incapable of being satisfied or appeased: insatiable hunger for knowledge.

intellect (IN-tel-ekt) Capacity for thinking and acquiring knowledge, especially of a high or complex sort. Large mental capacity.

keel (KEEL) A central fore-and-aft structural member in the bottom of a hull, extending from the stem to the sternpost and having the floors or frames attached to it, usually at right angles.

mechanics (mih-KA-niks) Workers who are skilled in the use of tools, machines, and equipment.

modifications (mah-deh-feh-KAY-shunz) Changes.

prominent (PRAH-meh-nent) Leading, important, or well known: a prominent citizen.

propelled (preh-PELD) Driven or caused to move, forward or onward: a boat propelled by rowing.

prototype (PROH-teh-typ) The original or model on which something is based or formed.

pseudonym (SOO-duh-nim) A fictitious name used by a person to conceal his or her identity.

Quaker (KWAY-kur) A popular name for a member of the religious Society of Friends.

redoubled (ree-DUH-buld) Doubled or made twice as great: to redouble one's efforts.

refurbished (ree-FUR-bished) Made like new, redone, brightened: to refurbish the lobby.

republican (rih-PUH-blih-ken) Favoring or support-
ing a nation in which the head of government is not
a monarch or other hereditary head of state.

sloop (SLOOP) A single-masted vessel with fore-and-
aft sails.

stern wheel (STERN WHEEL) A paddle wheel at the
rear of a ship.

subordinate (suh-BOR-dih-net) Placed in or belonging
to a lower order or rank, of less importance or inferior.

survey (sur-VAY) To determine the exact form, boundaries, position, and extent of a tract of land or section
of a country by linear and angular measurements and
by using geometry and trigonometry.

Tory (TOR-ee) A person who supported the British cause
in the American Revolution, a loyalist.

Additional Resources

To learn more about Robert Fulton, check out these books and Web sites:

Books

Flammang, James M. *Robert Fulton: Inventor and Steamboat Builder.* Berkeley Heights, NJ: Enslow Publishers, 1999.

Kroll, Steven. *Robert Fulton: From Submarine to Steamboat.* New York: Holiday House, 1999.

Philip, Cynthia Owen. *Robert Fulton: A Biography.* New York: Franklin Watts, 1985.

Schaefer, Lola M. *Robert Fulton.* Mankato, MN: Pebble Books, 2000.

Web Sites

http://archive.ncsa.uiuc.edu/Cyberia/RiverWeb/
    Projects/Ambot/TECH/TECH5.htm
http://web.mit.edu/invent/www/inventorsA-H/
    fulton.html

Bibliography

Books:

Dangerfield, George. *Chancellor Robert R. Livingston of New York, 1746-1813*. New York: Harcourt, Brace, 1960.

Dickinson, Henry W. *Robert Fulton: Engineer and Artist, His Life and Works*. London: John Lane, 1913.

Ford, Arthur Lewis. *Joel Barlow*. New York: Twayne Publishers, 1971.

Sale, Kirkpatrick. *The Fire of His Genius: Robert Fulton and the American Dream*. New York: Free Press, 2001.

Woodress, James. *A Yankee's Odyssey: The Life of Joel Barlow*. New York: Greenwood Press, 1958.

Works by Fulton:

A Treatise on the Improvement of Canal Navigation. London: I. & J. Taylor, 1796.

Plan for Supplying the City of New York with Fuel. New York: The New York Coal Company, 1814.

Report on the Proposed Canal between the Rivers Heyl and Helford. London: 1796.

Torpedo War and Submarine Explosions. New York: 1810.

Index

A

American Philosophical Society, 19, 52
American Revolution, 5, 14, 16, 19, 77

B

Barlow, Joel, 35, 86, 93
Bonaparte, Napoléon, 35, 42, 44, 46–47, 61–62
Boston Massacre, 14
Boston Tea Party, 14
Boulton and Watt, 31, 51, 60, 62, 66, 71
Braddock, General Edward, 11
Bridgewater, duke of, 27
Bridgewater Canal, 29
Bude Canal, 29
Bushnell, David, 39, 42

C

Calla, Étienne, 56, 60–61
Car of Neptune, 86, 89
Charles V, king of Spain, 49
Colles, Christopher, 19
Columbian Maid, 51–52
Continental Congress, 15, 55
Courtenay, Viscount William, 25, 27, 29

D

Dorothea, 69
Drebbel, Cornelis, 39

E

Ellicott, Andrew, 75
Embargo Act, 83
Erie Canal, 97

F

Firefly, 92
Fitch, John, 19, 50, 52–53, 55
Franklin, Benjamin, 18–19, 22
French and Indian War, 11
French Conservatory of Arts and Trades, 61
French Revolution, 5, 35
Fulton, Belle (sister), 7
Fulton, Betsey (sister), 7
Fulton, Cornelia (daughter), 93
Fulton, Juliet (daughter), 90
Fulton, Polly (sister), 7, 95
Fulton, Robert (son), 95
Fulton I, 95–96
Fulton II, 96
Fulton Sr., Robert (father), 5, 7–10

G

Gallatin, Albert, 83, 85
Garay, Blasco de, 49
George III, king of England, 11

H

Hamilton, Alexander, 34
Henry, William, 11, 23, 49
Hope, 91–93
Hulls, Jonathan, 49

J

Jefferson, President Thomas, 55, 75, 83, 86
Jersey, 92–93
Johnson, Caleb, 10, 14–15
Juliana Library, 7, 11, 49

L

Little Juliana, 73
Livingston, Robert R., 53, 55,
    57, 73, 75–76, 80, 82,
    85–86, 88, 91–94

M

Madison, James, 86
Mississippi River, 11, 55, 61,
    75, 89–91, 94
Mute, 94

N

Napoleonic Wars, 63
Nautilus, 42, 44, 46–48, 56, 60
Newcomen, Thomas, 49
New Orleans, 91–92
North River Steam Boat,
    81–83, 85–86, 88, 90–92,
    94

P

Paine, Thomas, 14, 19
Paragon, 91
Passages des Panoramas, 43
patent(s), 29, 31, 37, 49, 72,
    75, 86, 95
Peale, Charles Willson, 18, 23
Périer, Auguste Charles, 43,
    46, 61
Perseverance, 91–92
Phoenix, 85, 89–90
Polacca, 53
Pontcysyllte Aqueduct, 31, 33
Proclamation Line, 11, 14

R

Raritan, 86, 89
Rittenhouse, David, 14
Robert Fulton Birthplace
    museum, 8
Royal Academy of Arts, 24–25

Royal Society for the
    Encouragement of Arts,
    Manufactures and
    Commerce, 26
Rumsey, James, 21, 50–52

S

Smith, Mary (mother), 7, 10,
    22, 24
Stanhope, Earl, 27, 29
Stevens, John, 53, 55, 73,
    85–86

T

*Torpedo War and Submarine
    Explosions*, 90
Tory(ies), 10, 15
*Treatise on the Improvement
    of Canal Navigation, A*,
    33, 43
Turtle, 39, 42

W

War of 1812, 93
Washington, George, 19, 21,
    33–34
Watt, James, 50
West, Benjamin, 22, 35

About the Author

Dr. Morris A. Pierce served in the U.S. Army in Vietnam before graduating from the United States Military Academy at West Point, where he was trained as an engineer. After working as an engineer for several years, he received his doctorate in history from the University of Rochester in 1993. In addition to teaching history at the University of Rochester, he manages the University's energy management program and develops alternative energy production systems to reduce energy costs. Dr. Pierce has done extensive research on the history of energy and transportation, and maintains an extensive Web site about steam engines and the Erie Canal.

Credits

Photo Credits

Cover: Portrait: courtesy Independence National Historical; Inset: © Culver Pictures

Pp. 4, 54, 84 courtesy Independence National Historical Park; pp. 6, 58-59, 76, 79 © Library of Congress Geography and Map Division; pp. 8, 9 courtesy the Phelps Stokes Collection, Miriam and Ira D. Wallach Division of Art, Prints, and Photographs, the New York Public Library, Astor Lenox, and Tilden Foundations; p. 12 © Corbis; pp. 15, 20, 50, 65, 88 courtesy Rare Books and Manuscripts, the New York Public Library, Astor Lenox, and Tilden Foundations; pp. 16, 32 courtesy Hanford Collection, New York Public Library, Astor Lenox, and Tilden Foundations; p. 18 courtesy Museum of the City of New York, Gift of Estate of Julia Stuyvesant Winterhoff through Fannie G. Dudley; p. 21 © Tate Gallery, London/Art Resource, NY; pp. 24, 51, 92 © Culver Pictures; p. 25 © Jeremy Horner/CORBIS; p. 27 © Michael Nicholson/CORBIS; pp. 28, 36 © Prints George; p. 30 *Robert Fulton papers "Report on the Proposed Canal...",* Manuscripts and Archives Division, New York Public Library, Astor Lenox, and Tilden Foundations; p. 38 © National Portrait Gallery, Smithsonian Institution/Art Resource, NY; pp. 39, 47 courtesy U.S. Naval Historical Center; pp. 40-41, 81 courtesy Manuscripts and Archives Division, the New York Public Library, Astor Lenox, and Tilden Foundations; p. 44 © Harald A. Jahn; Viennaslide Photoagency/CORBIS; p. 45 © Musée Nat. du Chateau de Malmaison, Rueil-Malmaison/Lauros-Giraudon, Paris/SuperStock; pp. 52, 57, 68 © Bettmann/Corbis; p. 53 © Library of Congress Prints and Photographs Division; p. 64 © Gianni Dagli Orti/CORBIS; p. 67 (upper right) © Baldwin H. Ward & Kathryn C. Ward/CORBIS; p. 70 © Archivo Iconografico, S.A./CORBIS; pp. 74, 74 inset Cindy Reiman; p. 77 the Bayley Collection, Mariner's Museum, Newport News, VA; p. 87 © Library of Congress Geography and Map Division, Washington, D.C., G3300 1776 .M52 Vault; p. 96 © Lee Snider; Lee Snider/CORBIS; p. 98 © Museum of the City of New York/CORBIS.

Editor Joanne Randolph

Series Design Laura Murawski

Layout Design Corinne Jacob

Photo Researcher Jeffrey Wendt